Seashells
IN MY POCKET

50 Ways to Live a Beach Inspired Life

JENNIFER MELVILLE

Copyright © 2022 Jennifer Melville
Illustrations © Elvira Silenkova
All rights reserved.
ISBN: 9798827695011

Dedication

For Nanny
Your love of the beach was contagious.

For Papa (aka Monkey)
Thank you for providing our family with
a magical place to connect.

Table of Contents

Dedication iii
Introduction ix

1. View Every Day as a Clean Slate 1
2. Dive Deeper 3
3. Soothe Yourself with Blue 6
4. Dine Al Fresco 8
5. Enjoy the Process 10
6. Embrace Beach Chic Style 12
7. Love the Earth 14
8. Age Gracefully 17
9. Escape Guilt Free 19
10. Don't Forget the Sunscreen 21
11. Let Go of Perfectionism 23
12. Surround Yourself with Water 25
13. Connect Casually 27
14. Surrender 29

15. Paint Your Toes Pretty 31
16. Practice Patience 33
17. Do Nothing 35
18. Wear Pearls 37
19. Weather Your Storms 38
20. Buy Some Beach in a Bottle 40
21. Disconnect 42
22. Connect With Your Inner Hermit Crab 44
23. Go Bronze 46
24. Clear the Air 48
25. Cool Off 50
26. Be a Beach Diva 52
27. Hunt for Treasure 54
28. Welcome More White 56
29. Embrace Your Inner Jellyfish 58
30. Pack Light 60
31. Go for a Windswept Look 62
32. Exfoliate 63
33. Take a Cinematic Adventure 65
34. Nap More 67
35. Seek Solitude 69

36. Plant a Beach Inspired Garden 71
37. Hydrate 73
38. Clear the Clutter 75
39. Grab a Life Preserver 77
40. Walk More 79
41. Sprinkle Your Home in Coastal Décor 81
42. Dry Your Clothes on the Line 83
43. Enjoy Lighter Meals 85
44. Ebb and Flow with Grace 87
45. Travel by Book 89
46. Create Mystery 91
47. Sleep Deeply 93
48. Eat High Quality Ice Cream 95
49. Get Outside 97
50. Immerse Yourself 99

Bonus: Find Joy in Simplicity 101
A Note from The Author 103
Other Books by Jennifer Melville 105
About the Author 107

Introduction

Hello! Thank you so much for picking up this little book of mine. My guess is you probably chose this title because you love the beach as much as I do! We aren't alone. The beach is a beautiful, magical, transformative and intriguing place that holds a special place in the hearts of many.

I've been fortunate enough to live near the ocean all my life, and it never gets old. In fact, the more time I spend at the seashore, the more I cherish it, and the deeper the bond grows. Whenever I find myself standing on a beach, I feel a sense of awe and wonder wash over me. It is a place I seek to reset, relax and recharge. Time spent at the beach is both calming *and* invigorating.

My house here in Nova Scotia is located a mere five hundred feet from the Atlantic Ocean. Yes, I live within walking distance of a beautiful beach! That being said, I'm only human, and I don't always appreciate or take advantage of the beauty and wonder outside my doorstep. I get caught up in the struggles, demands and pressures of everyday life just as much as anybody—work, appointments, homework help, chauffeuring children, errands, social commitments…etc.

Although I live in a coastal community, it is my annual trips to our family's seaside cottage that allow me to connect most intimately with the beach. During this one week a year, I live and breathe the beach, in both a literal and figurative sense! Our cottage sits on the golden sands of Youghall Beach, overlooking the beautiful Baie des Chaleurs in the province of New Brunswick, Canada. This piece of land has been in the family for generations. In 2004, my grandfather tore down the original cottage on the property and built a new one that could accommodate his growing clan of children, grandchildren and great-grandchildren. He had a vision to create a special place we could all return to each summer, to reunite with our roots and connect with each other. I always depart our little cottage with a heavy heart, and a deep longing to bottle up the essence of the beach to take home with me.

That's what this book represents. It is a compilation of the notes and musings I've jotted down over the years during my beachside cottage vacations. I've learned that living a beach inspired life elevates the experience of each day, whether you live near the ocean, visit it occasionally, or have never stepped foot on its sandy shores. My hope is that by sharing my thoughts, you too can carry a few seashells in your pocket wherever you may go, sprinkling each day with a dash of beach magic.

This book is meant to be an easy, breezy read and a petite source of inspiration that you can reach for anytime and anywhere you crave a dose of beachy goodness. Read it in the summer while lazing on a beach blanket. Read it in the dead of winter when you need a little pick me up. Read it from start to finish or choose a couple of chapters at random.

Are you ready to go beachcombing with me to hunt for hidden nuggets of inspiration? Grab your swimsuit, towel and sunglasses (don't forget the sunscreen) and let's get going! I'll race you to the shore…

1

View Every Day as a Clean Slate

Despite the fact I'm on vacation, I always rise with the birds (sometimes before) when I'm staying at this little beachside cottage. I don't want to waste a single minute of the few precious days a year I'm fortunate enough to spend here. I've always been a morning person, but there is something particularly magical about this time of day on the beach. The rise and fall of the tide while the world slept wiped the slate clean in a very literal sense. I love the idea of being up and out the door before anyone else, making the first tracks of the day on the smooth, clean, hard sand; wiping away the mistakes of yesterday and creating fresh, new and exciting patterns.

View each and every day as a clean slate. Imagine the stress, worries and mistakes of yesterday have been wiped clean by ocean waves and carried out to sea! Each day represents a new beginning to start fresh with your goals, your relationships, your mindset and your behaviors.

Begin each morning with a moment to contemplate your intention for the day. What first tracks do you want to make today? I keep a small journal on my coffee table for this very purpose. It only takes a couple of minutes to jot down my daily intention each morning, but it is a powerful habit that helps me start each day with that clean slate mindset.

2

Dive Deeper

If you read comic books growing up as I did, you might remember the old advertisements for Sea-Monkeys. Those ads were certainly enticing, and very effective. I was one of the suckers who spent my piggy bank money on my very own colony of Sea-Monkeys. I'm sure I wasn't the only kid who was thoroughly disappointed that my new pets (which were not monkeys, but actually brine shrimp) looked absolutely nothing like the humanoid creatures depicted on the packaging. I was envisioning a magical underwater kingdom of mythical creatures and mermaids, instead of a few clear little crustaceans with an incredibly short life span. Despite my unpleasant Sea-Monkey experience, I've always been fascinated with the unseen community of sea life that hides below the water's surface.

I think it's natural for humans to be mystified by the secrets of the ocean. When my kids were little, one of their favorite beach activities was "goggling". This was their word for snorkeling! They were (and still are as teens) completely enthralled with the bustling world that came into view when they slipped their heads below the surface.

From my post on this lounge chair, I sit back and admire the vast blanket of blue that stretches out before me. It's incredible to think that just under the surface is a whole different world, teaming with life, activity and mysteries to solve.

Don't just scratch the surface. Instead of accepting things at face value, choose to dive deeper and open your eyes and mind to what hides underneath. Approach life with curiosity! Ask tons of questions. Research topics that pique your interest and take things to the next level.

The next time you have a conversation with someone (a good friend, acquaintance or stranger), make a point of being inquisitive and a good listener. Ask questions that extend beyond the standbys, "How are you? Can you believe this weather?" Connect with people on a deeper and more meaningful level.

3

Soothe Yourself with Blue

There's something incredibly soothing about being enveloped in blue, the prominent color on the beach. The sea and the sky shimmer and shift in varying shades of blue ranging from the soft pale hue of the morning mist, to the rich deep tone of twilight. Apparently, I'm not alone in my love of blue. Surveys show that it is one of the most favored colors and is associated with feelings of peace, tranquility and calm. This isn't surprising, as I can literally feel the stress drain from my body as I revel in the sight of the expansive blue space before me.

Look for ways to invite more blue into your surroundings. You don't have to live by the ocean to do this! Think of those spaces of your home where you like to seek refuge and unwind. My bedroom serves as my great escape. I painted the walls a soft, soothing and luminous blue that is reminiscent of cool, misty morning walks along the shore. (If you are interested, it's called *Beacon Grey 2128-60* by Benjamin Moore.) Blue is a wonderful choice for a bathroom. I have a friend who actually painted the ceiling of her bathroom blue. Isn't that a fabulous idea? She can pretend she's gazing at the sky as she relaxes in the bathtub.

If you aren't big on pulling out the paint and roller, brainstorm a list of tiny ways to add a splash of blue to your life. Fluffy towels, crisp cool sheets, an airy blouse and pretty throw cushions are all great options. Set your phone home screen to a watery blue image. Open your blinds and curtains so you can see the sky!

4

Dine Al Fresco

Beach snacks are usually simple and straightforward—a refreshing glass of lemonade, a humble PB&J sandwich, a juicy slice of watermelon, a bag of satisfyingly salty chips. When navigating sand dunes and hauling coolers, simplicity is a necessity. That being said, no matter what I nibble on at the beach, it feels decadently delicious. I think it has something to do with the novelty of dining al fresco. Food just seems to *taste better* when paired with fresh salty air and a relaxed casual atmosphere.

Enjoy al fresco dining whenever the opportunity strikes! I know it's easier and more convenient to sit at the handy kitchen table, but moving your dining experience outside is worth the extra effort. We have a small picnic table on our deck, so it's really quite easy to grab the plates and cutlery and head outdoors. During the summer months, my favorite time of day is when I get to enjoy my morning oatmeal and tea on the deck, while listening to the birds and watching the sun rise. Don't rule out al fresco dining during the winter months either. Hot cocoa always tastes better when you are plunked in a snowbank.

5

Enjoy the Process

The other day I watched a couple of children build an elaborate system of sandcastles and moats. It was practically a medieval village! I haven't built a sandcastle in years, but seeing their joy gave me an itch to grab a shovel and pail. I have such fond memories of spending hours on the sandbars creating castles and spaceships, lost in my own little world of make-believe. (I usually cast myself as Princess Leia and my cousin was Luke Skywalker.)

Building sandcastles is about the creative process more than the final product. Despite the time and effort we put in, we know with certainty that our creations will be swept away when the next high tide rolls around. Our castle must surrender to the tide. There is no other option. Sandcastles remind us to focus on the present and loosen our grip on the future or the final product.

I truly love writing my books, but every now and then I feel a sense of impatience creeping into my psyche. I find myself rushing to complete a project… and for what? It is the creative process I find most fulfilling, and the final product is really the icing on the cake.

Do you find yourself rushing through things to tick another item off your to-do list? This sense of urgency really adds an unnecessary layer of stress to life. Try to slow yourself down and view the *act of doing as the reward*, instead of the completed project. Keep the mantra, "process over product" top of mind as you go about your day. Marvel at the freshness and bright colors of the vegetables you are chopping for dinner. Snuggle up to the warmth of the towels you are folding, straight from the dryer. Appreciate the one-on-one time you get to spend with your child while helping them with their homework. (Note to self while tutoring my son in grade 10 math and pre-calculus.)

6

Embrace Beach Chic Style

Packing for a trip to the beach is as easy as it gets. There is no room in your suitcase or tote bag for fussy, heavy or complicated attire. I live in my bathing suit, sundresses and oversized cover-ups. Shoes are optional and usually unnecessary. When it's chilly, I opt for wide-leg linen pants and a classic seaside inspired striped cotton sweater (or a marinière as they are called in France).

Beach style has an air of easy breeziness that centers around casual comfort and simplicity. You don't have to be visiting the beach to embrace a casually chic look. Why not bring that lighthearted, care-free vibe into your wardrobe at home? (No, I'm not suggesting we walk around our homes in a bikini.) Wear dresses more often. They are so easy to slip on with little thought or effort. Choose soft, airy and natural fabrics such as cotton and linen that will keep you cool and won't stick to your skin. Don't worry about the wrinkles! Embrace a tousled, relaxed style. Choose styles and cuts that are slightly oversized and don't restrict your movement. Give your body room to breathe and stretch out in comfort.

7

Love the Earth

I never miss a walk on the sandbars when low tide rolls around. Every day is a new adventure because I never know what little discovery awaits in the shallow waters of the tidepools. Moon snails creep along the sandy bottom. Tiny tickle fish dart between my toes. Crabs scuttle sideways, trying to evade capture by the gulls (or curious children). If I'm lucky, I might spot a rare sand dollar or starfish. I'm continuously amazed and in awe of the sheer abundance and interconnectedness of life on this planet.

Do your part in caring for this precious planet. We are all in this together. I don't pretend to be an eco-warrior, but there are so many easy ways to act and live more sustainably. All our small efforts combined can add up to have a big impact. Buy less stuff, shop second-hand, be mindful of your water consumption, consolidate your errands to conserve fuel, shop local, compost your kitchen scraps, carpool, dry your clothes on the line, choose eco-friendly cleaning products…etc. The options are limitless. Pick one new environmentally friendly habit to implement today! Feel good about doing your part to protect the planet.

8

Age Gracefully

The coastal environment is not for the faint of heart. Inhabitants of the beach take a beating from the elements. Surf, sun, sand, salt and wind each leave their mark. What I find fascinating is the beauty that emerges from the weathering process. I love collecting interesting pieces of driftwood on my beach walks. Each one is unique and some of them look as if they were deliberately sculpted into a work of art. Only time and wear can create such authentic character, depth, patina and substance.

There is beauty in aging. I'm guessing most of us could use this reminder (myself included). We often lament our grey hair, wrinkles and sagging skin, and do everything in our power to fight the inevitable. I vote we shift our mindset and choose to accept the aging process with grace and gratitude. I'm not proposing we throw out our serums, face creams or hair dyes. I'm just suggesting that when we look in the mirror each morning, we celebrate the fact that we've made it this far!

Speak kindly to yourself. Remind yourself that wrinkles, sunspots, freckles and greying hair are a symbol of your own authenticity and a life well lived. You are wiser than you were in your youth! Honestly, I'm happier, more confident and more self-assured in my late forties than I was in my twenties. I don't think I would trade this inner sense of contentment for a smoother, plumper complexion.

9

Escape Guilt Free

Have you ever checked a book out from a one of those free little libraries in your community? They seem to be popping up everywhere, and I'm not surprised by their popularity. We have a similar set up at our family cottage in a corner of one of the bedrooms. Our cottage is owned by four families who rotate in and out on a schedule. When someone is finished with one of their beach reads, they often leave it behind for the next visitor to enjoy. There's nothing heavy or overly intellectual on the bookshelf, which suits me just fine. I love indulging in light, frivolous (sometimes racy) literature. Afterall, when I'm at the beach, I'm looking to escape!

I know many of us are trying to expand our minds and challenge our intellect, but that doesn't mean we shouldn't indulge in fantasy on a regular basis. Don't save the trashy beach reads for the beach! Read them whenever it suits you, and enjoy every delicious morsel guilt free. If you feel embarrassed to reveal your reading selection to others, download an eBook on your tablet or Kindle. Indulge discreetly!

10

Don't Forget the Sunscreen

I can relate to getting caught up in a sense of overzealous enthusiasm at the sight of the beach; throwing all cares and worries aside. It's easy to forget the sunscreen when all we want to do is run to the shore and dip our toes in the water. Before we know it, we are fried to a bright lobster red, and are forced to end the fun to seek shade and shelter. Unfortunately, I've had more than my fair share of sunburns.

Make a habit of applying sunscreen *every single day of the year*, rain or shine, summer, winter, spring or fall. (I received my worst sunburn ever in the winter, horseback riding all day on snowy fields.) It's a healthy habit that everyone should adopt. Not only does it protect our skin from the harm of the sun's rays, but it also prevents wrinkles and pigmentation marks.

(Yes, I'm fully aware I suggested we embrace said wrinkles and spots, but if applying sunscreen reduces them, I'll take the win.)

I take a multi-layered approach to ensure I'm well covered. I apply a sheer 45 SPF cream under my make-up, but my mineral foundation also carries an SPF rating of 25. (I'm a fan of *Glow Time Full Coverage Mineral BB Cream* by Jane Iredale.) Throughout the day I touch up my protection with a translucent sunscreen powder. (I use another Jane Iredale product called *Powder-Me SPF 30 Dry Sunscreen*.) I'm less picky about my body and use whatever product we have on hand around the house to slather on exposed areas of skin. (By the way, I should mention that I have no affiliations with any of the products or brands I mention in this book. I just enjoy sharing my favorites!)

11

Let Go of Perfectionism

Beaches can be messy and disorderly places. Pounding surf hauls in debris and litters it across the sand. The smell of decomposition hangs in the air after a large storm. The beach doesn't aim for perfection, cleanliness and symmetry as so many of us do. It takes a more care-free approach to housekeeping by relying on the natural ebb and flow of the tides to look after the details.

Life is messy, and I think far too many women spend far too much time fretting over keeping their homes and lives in tip top shape. I'll be the first to admit that I love a sparkling clean and uncluttered home, but the reality is, I live with two teenage boys. (Yes, there are times I feel like I'm living with a bunch of messy college roommates I didn't sign up for. I have a nacho factory running in my kitchen 24/7.) It is a losing battle to keep the house as clean, neat and tidy as I would like, so I have decided to let go of perfectionism. The truth is, I have many things I'd like to spend time on, and although I don't mind cleaning, there comes a point where enough is enough. I pick and choose those areas that are important to me, and I turn a blind eye to the rest.

Designate certain areas of your home as top priority. Keep these areas in a state of sparkling order and forget the rest. I suggest choosing an area you have a lot of control over, like your own bedroom, or a space you spend a lot of time in, such as the kitchen. Use the time you used to spend tidying and cleaning to explore one of your passions in life.

12

Surround Yourself with Water

When I'm at the cottage, I always sleep with the windows open. I love falling asleep to the sound of waves. The steady, rhythmic sound is both soothing and reassuring. Our cottage is located right on the beach, but back home our house is set about five hundred feet from the shoreline. The sound of the ocean does travel if the wind is right. It's usually more of roar as we are located on the open Atlantic.

It doesn't matter if you don't live near the water's edge. There are lots of little ways to bring the therapeutic sound of water into your life. You too can be lulled to sleep by the rhythm of the sea. All you have to do is download a "waves" track from iTunes or

Spotify and you can drift off to sea and dreamland at the same time. My mother has a little indoor fountain in her bedroom that she runs occasionally. It produces a pleasant sound that is reminiscent of a babbling brook. You can pick one of these up at a garden center, homewares store or, of course, good old Amazon!

13

Connect Casually

When low tide hits and the sandbars emerge, the beach comes alive. I like to think of it as an informal happy hour of sorts. It's a tradition for people to walk the bars and connect with each other in a casual and informal manner. Growing up, I used to love tagging along with my grandmother on her walks. She was quite a social butterfly, and I enjoyed eavesdropping on her jovial and lively conversations with friends and neighbors.

I think we could all use a bit more face-to-face connection these days. Social distancing has taken a toll on our relationships. I love the informal and spontaneous nature of seaside socializing. It suits my introverted nature. I used to beat myself up for not entertaining enough. It was one of those things I thought

I *should* do. (My mother is, and grandmother was, a master of dinner parties.) The truth is, I don't enjoy having people over, and I've come to realize that's ok. I much prefer the beach style approach to connecting with others.

Get out in your community and go for a walk in the evening instead of watching TV. Stop and catch up with your neighbours and say hello to strangers passing by. Lately I've been meeting up with the same woman and her two sweet dogs every morning on my run. I don't even know her name, but I enjoy engaging in a bit of small talk and lapping up doggy kisses and cuddles.

14

Surrender

It is nearly impossible to go to the beach and not get sand in every crack and crevice of your body. If you remembered your sunscreen (of course you did!) you have basically turned yourself into a sand magnet. Yes, it can feel a bit icky and uncomfortable, but why waste your time trying to fight it? Surrender yourself to the sand and you will be much more content and carefree. You can always rinse off at the showers in the parking lot and have a proper bath when you get home to get those hard-to-reach places.

There are times in life when surrendering and opting for the path of least resistance makes the most sense. Instead of fighting the inevitable, enjoy the magic of the present moment. Why make yourself miserable fretting over all the things in life that you can't control?

I've been thinking about the word surrender in the context of relationships lately. I used to want to control or change people to suit me, but I've realized this is simply impossible! Are there people in your life that irritate you? Surrender to the fact that they are who they are. It's not your job to try to change them. You can choose to accept them as is and decide for yourself how much time you wish to spend with them.

15

Paint Your Toes Pretty

Shoes are really just an inconvenience at the beach, so you might as well go without. I prefer to walk the shoreline barefoot and fancy free! Of course, I like my feet to look pretty and presentable, and colorful toes are a must. Classic red is my go-to color.

Look after your feet year-round, not just during sandal season. Even if they are wrapped up in woolen socks and winter boots, it feels special and uplifting to have well-groomed feet. Pretty toes are one of life's small pleasures!

During the summer, I treat myself to professional pedicures once a month. The technicians at the spa work magic with their polish applications! The rest of the year, I adopt a do-it-yourself approach. Once or twice a week I use a file on any rough spots and apply a heavy-duty foot cream afterwards. (I love the Gehwol line of products.) I often use a nail strengthening polish during the winter to give my toenails a boost after a hard-working summer. (I like *Nail Envy* by OPI.)

16

Practice Patience

I've been collecting pieces of sea glass all my life. They hold the status of precious gems in my family. The rarer the color, the more valuable the piece. Blue, purple, pink and red are high-ticket items.

I'll never forget the day we hit the sea glass jackpot on a family trip to Barbados. It was near the famous surf break called "Soup Bowl". There was sea glass to be found at every step. Oddly enough, it was the same day that Kelly Slater (eleven-time world champion) was surfing there. While my husband (a surfer), was starstruck, my kids could have cared less about this celebrity siting! They were too busy collecting hidden gems to even notice.

Sea glass teaches us patience. One of the things that makes sea glass so intriguing is the length of time it takes to create it. Nature needs to work its magic for as much as thirty years, and in many cases even longer. It's a process that cannot be rushed.

Where could you exercise more patience in your life? Maybe you need to chill out a bit more in heavy traffic. (I'm raising my hand on this one!) Maybe you need to practice more patience with your children, and trust that they will mature and grow at a rate that is just right for them. Perhaps you need to give *yourself* more grace. Just like a piece of sea glass churning in the ocean, you are a work-in-progress that takes time to evolve. Don't put too much pressure on yourself to achieve all your goals in one fell swoop. Practice patience with yourself and allow time to work its magic.

17

Do Nothing

Life on the beach moves at a slower pace. The days feel long, languid and luxurious. No one looks down their nose at being lazy and unproductive at the beach. Sitting still and doing nothing is both expected and celebrated.

Do nothing more often! Hit pause on the treadmill of productivity. Set aside time each and every day to just sit and be. It doesn't have to be anything formal like a meditation practice (unless you want to). Take five or ten minutes completely to yourself with no distractions present. Resist the urge to pick up your phone, flip open a book or turn on the TV.

I notice that the more space I allow for doing nothing, the more creativity I discover within. When I allow myself time to clear my mind and sit uninterrupted, I'm able to ponder, think and create my own inspiration.

If you need a little inspiration on this topic, I recommend the book, *The Sweetness of Doing Nothing: Live Life the Italian Way With Dolce Far Niente* by Sophie Minchilli. It sounds like the Italians have this concept figured out!

18

Wear Pearls

I've always been fascinated with pearls. Growing up, I used to collect mussels from the large rocks in front of our cottage. Did you know that the wild blue mussel produces tiny pearls? They are nothing like the commercially raised pearls used in jewelry. Although quite miniscule, they are still shiny and pretty, and were fun to collect as a child.

Dig out your pearls and wear them! Pearls are a timeless classic that will never go out of style. They add a decadent touch of the sea to any outfit, no matter the time of year. I really like some of the modern options that jewelry designers are offering lately. I have a pair of gold hoops with a large baroque pearl hanging from each. The irregular shape of these pearls suits my casual style. My earrings are a nice blend of modern and classic.

19

Weather Your Storms

Beach days are not all blue skies and rainbows. The sea is moody and expresses its emotions with passion. What I've noticed is that the ocean retains its beauty, no matter the weather. I love the everchanging landscape of texture and color that shifts with the conditions of the day. Some of my favorite moments on the beach have taken place during wild thunderstorms. Storms display a captivating show for the senses with their dark ominous clouds, crackling lightning and earth-shaking thunder.

What if we too could find beauty in our darkest moments? Embrace your bad moods and negative emotions. It's not healthy to expect to feel sunny all the time. Be kind, accepting and patient with yourself when you hit rough seas. Grab the closest life preserver, and when you make it to safety, ask what you can gain from the experience. Maybe your painful divorce led to more independence and a greater sense of self. Maybe an illness showed you how strong and resilient you are in body and mind. There is a silver lining to life's most difficult challenges, you just have to search for it.

20

Buy Some Beach in a Bottle

What is it about the scent of sunscreen that is so appealing? I still remember fondly the smell of Hawaiian Tropic #4 Tanning Oil from my youth. (And I wonder why I had so many sunburns growing up!) There is something yummy and nostalgic about this cocktail of tropical scents that transports me back in time to lazy and leisurely beach days.

When you find yourself longing for the beach, why not indulge in a little aromatherapy? I enjoy wearing beach inspired scents all year long. My current favorite is called *Vanori* by Sylvaine Delacourte. In the company's own words, "Vanori suggests a mirage calling you to an imaginary island. It takes you on a boat to discover endless magical beaches and whispers sweet words of escape to unknown and exotic places. Vanori is generous and sunny. Its shining face is surrounded by magnificent flowers that embrace you as they mingle with the sensuality of vanilla." Ok, I have to admit, whoever wrote this description is a master at marketing.

Discover your own beach-themed signature scent. A quick Google search will point you in the right direction. From there have fun trying samples at your closest Sephora or department store.

If perfume isn't your thing, choose a bath or shower gel with a tropical vibe. You can't go wrong with something that includes coconut, mango, watermelon, mint or citrus scents. Yum!

21

Disconnect

It's easy to lose track of time on the beach. We live by the sun instead of our watches (or I guess our smartphones these days). Time meanders along at an unhurried pace as we lose touch with the hectic world back home. WIFI is not missed, nor are the real time updates of breaking news from every corner of the planet. When you are at the beach, all that matters is the here and now.

Disconnecting from reality is effortless when surrounded by the magnificence of the sea. Whenever I visit the cottage, I put myself on a voluntary news fast, which is actually pretty easy to stick to! I'm really not tempted to pick up my phone and tune in to the outside world. Sadly, such is not the case when I return back to the reality of day-to-day life. Reading the news can be addictive, as the headlines are designed to keep you coming back from more.

News fasts are a great way to transport yourself into a dreamy, beachy state of mind. I've started incorporating them regularly into my life and they have made a huge impact on reducing my stress levels. I'm not suggesting we disconnect completely. There is a lot going on in the world right now, and it's important to be informed. That being said, you don't need to know everything the minute it unfolds. Choose a period of time that suits your lifestyle to unplug from current events. I like to start my fasts on Friday evening and let them stretch through to the end of the weekend.

22

Connect With Your Inner Hermit Crab

I love hermit crabs. Not only are they cute, they are also very clever! While gastropods such as snails grow their own shells when they are in need of a new one, hermit crabs let others put in all the hard work. They move into the discarded shells of other animals. How resourceful is that?

I wrote a book called *Preloved Chic* that discusses how to build a fabulous wardrobe out of second-hand clothing. The hermit crab has been living and breathing a preloved chic lifestyle for millions of years! You too can tap into your inner hermit crab by embracing a second-hand mindset. The next time you want to purchase something, seek out the available options on the preloved market. Not only will you save money, but you will also be consuming in a more sustainable manner. Clothing, sporting gear, furniture, housewares, electronics, toys, books…the possibilities are endless.

23

Go Bronze

I know I made a strong case for sunscreen earlier, but I do have to admit that I love the look of a good tan. Tanned skin has a healthy sun-kissed glow. It suggests a person is active, outdoorsy and living the good life! As the old saying goes, "Life is better with a tan."

Sadly, we all know this isn't really the case. While a real suntan might look good, it's *not good for you*! There is apparently no such thing as a healthy tan, because any change in your skin color is considered sun damage.

Sigh! What's a girl to do? Buy your tan in a bottle of course! If you love the look as much as I do, then find yourself a good quality self-tanner. Some of them can leave you looking a little orange, so be sure to test it out on an inconspicuous spot before you commit. My favorite is Topicrem's *Ultra-Moisturizing Progressive Tan*, which I picked up on my last visit to France. It's hard to find on my side of the pond, so I've also used *Natural Glow Daily Moisturizer* by Jergens. It's a basic drugstore brand but I've been very happy with the results. Be sure to give your skin a good exfoliation in the shower with a loofah before applying any product to ensure an even application of color.

Another great way to add a sun-kissed glow is by using a bronzing powder. You don't have to go crazy with it, as the idea is not to replicate a full-face tan. A light sweep along your cheekbones, the bridge of your nose and around the perimeter of your face should do the trick.

24

Clear the Air

Coastal fog is common during the summer months. The combination of the warm air with the cool sea water is a recipe for pea soup. Many mornings at the cottage I peek outside the window to see a thick bank of fog blanketing everything in sight (or I guess out of sight). This, however, is usually no indication of how the weather will unfold that day. By mid-morning the fog usually burns off, and I get to enjoy another golden day in this salty, sandy haven.

Often, our initial knee-jerk reaction in many situations is to assume the worst. Jumping to conclusions and misunderstanding situations can lead to further conflict. Why not clear the fog instead? If someone hurts your feelings, or says something that offends you, let them know how your feel, instead of letting your negative emotions fester into resentment. Clearing the air with someone can be liberating, and you'll often find that the person meant no harm with their comments, they were just misinterpreted.

My husband and I are both working on being more open and honest with each other about what we are thinking. The other day I said something that offended him, and my words came out much harsher than I intended. Instead of storming off in a huff, he told me how he felt, and I explained what I really intended to say. The air cleared between us, and we kissed and made up!

25

Cool Off

The body of water where our cottage sits is called the Baie des Chaleurs (which translates to warm bay in English.) Although the waters are considered warm by Canadian standards (they average around 18°C/64°F in August), most people might consider them a little on the chilly side. It goes without saying that a dip in these waters is refreshing and energizing—the perfect way to cool off on a hot day at the beach.

Sadly, we can't all hit the beach any time we need to cool off. Look for fun and creative ways to keep your cool (in the very literal sense) when the temperatures start to rise. Pop some ice in your water bottle and stay hydrated. Take a cold (or cool) bath or shower. Spritz yourself with a facial mist (My favorite is Avène's

Thermal Spring Water Mist.) Store your body cream in the refrigerator and slather yourself in refreshing luxury. Seek out air-conditioned spaces. Meal plan accordingly by choosing recipes that don't require the oven. Wash your car and get wet while you do it. Not only will you cool off, but you'll have a nice clean vehicle (win-win).

26

Be a Beach Diva

You don't have to sacrifice your sense of style when visiting the beach. I keep my accessories to a minimum during my seaside escapes, but there are two items I can't live without—my oversized sunglasses and my straw fedora. I can't think of a chicer combination!

Nothing says diva like an oversized pair of sunglasses. Find a pair that suits the shape of your face and wear them *everywhere* you go! My favorite style is the *Jacki Ohh* model made by Ray-Ban (and just like a hermit crab, I picked mine up preloved and in pristine condition on eBay).

I initially bought my straw hat to keep the sun off my face during a family vacation to the island of Guadeloupe. I fell in love with it, and when we returned from our trip, I didn't want to take it off. Straw hats add a beachy vacation vibe to any outfit. I wear mine all summer long no matter what I've got on the agenda for the day. If you aren't keen on hats, another option is a straw bag.

27

Hunt for Treasure

I've been a beachcomber all my life. As children, my sister and I spent countless hours hunting the shores near our cottage for treasure. We were usually on the lookout for shells, sea glass and fossils to add to our ever-growing collection, but anything was up for grabs. My sister once came home with a dead squid to dissect. (I took a pass, and not surprisingly, she ended up studying marine biology at university.)

As an adult, I still keep a close eye on the ground in front of me. I rarely come home from a walk on the beach with empty pockets. In fact, my passion for beachcombing served as the inspiration for the title of this book! I realized how bringing home a few "seashells in my pocket" enables me to carry the beach in my heart at all times.

In my book *Elevate Your Life at Home,* I wrote a chapter titled *Invite Mother Nature in for a Visit.* Natural objects make beautiful home décor and serve as wonderful reminders of some of our favorite places. The next time you are out for a nature walk, slip a tiny memento in your pocket. When you get home, display it somewhere prominently so you can admire it on a regular basis. Of course, items don't need to be from the beach! I collect treasures on my walks in the woods as well. Some of my favorite precious finds include shells, sea glass, abandoned bird nests, feathers, pinecones, seed pods, interesting stones and fossils.

28

Welcome More White

When my firstborn was a baby, we used to recite the same poem to him each night at bedtime. It was written by the Canadian author Sheree Fitch and his favorite line was, "If I were the ocean, I'd sail you away, and bring you back home at the end of the day." (You can buy the entire poem in storybook form. It's called *If I Were the Moon*. The illustrations are beautiful and whimsical, and I guarantee you'll be crying by the time you get to the end.) Interestingly, my son ended up becoming an avid and skilled sailor at a very young age. I'm guessing his passion for boats was not a coincidence.

I'm not a sailor myself (I'm prone to terrible sea sickness), but I'm attracted to sailboats. There is something aesthetically pleasing about the sight of white sails dotting the blue landscape on a bright, sunny and windswept day. The juxtaposition of these two colors provides a stunning effect.

White might be the most understated of all colors, but it has a powerful impact. White is sparkling, clean, fresh, invigorating, pure, light and elegant. Seek out ways to capture the essence of those crisp white sails into your day-to-day life.

White on white is the ultimate color combination in my view. I went with this theme in my laundry room to capture a clean ambiance (white walls, white flooring, white appliances and white cabinetry). The room is fresh and bright, and I actually *enjoy* spending time in there!

Could a room in your house use a fresh coat of paint? You can't go wrong with white. It provides the perfect backdrop for artwork and wall hangings. (Have you noticed that gallery walls are always painted white?) Don't be shy to wear more white. A white cotton or linen shirt exudes a beachy vibe. Keep a detergent stick in your handbag to deal with any stains immediately. White sheets, white towels and white dinnerware have a luxurious look and feel. White is the new black!

29

Embrace Your Inner Jellyfish

Growing up, I was never a huge fan of jellyfish. In fact, I was petrified of them. I realize some species can be deadly, but the variety where we live (the artic red) is harmless, and more of a nuisance than anything. Lately on my beach walks, I've been viewing jellyfish through a different lens. They are in fact beautiful and interesting creatures. They come in varying shades that range from bright red to a deep rich purple. (I used to think they looked like grape jelly, but thankfully I never did a taste test.) Because they have very limited swimming ability, they travel by hitching a ride on ocean currents. They are masters of going with the flow!

Tap into the jellyfish mindset more often. Relax, chill out and go with the flow. Embrace flexibility and you'll likely be a happier person. I am a planner by nature. (I may even be classified as an over-planner.) Although being organized and prepared has many benefits, it can have a downside when the unexpected occurs. I tend to get frazzled if things don't go as I've mapped them out in my head. I've been working on this, and for me it comes down to taking a few minutes to recalibrate before jumping to conclusions or hitting the drama button. The next time you find yourself getting cranky by the unexpected, think jellyfish, not crab!

30

Pack Light

There is something liberating about leaving the bulk of your belongings behind and fitting everything you need into one tiny bag. I pack a light suitcase for my visits to the cottage. Beach attire is simple and uncomplicated, so I need very little to feel both happy and stylish.

Whenever I return from a vacation, I'm always blown away by how much stuff I own. It makes me question how much I truly need in life, since I clearly survived my recent trip with very little.

If you want to infuse a bit of that beach simplicity into your current life, pare down your wardrobe to a few select pieces. Choose what you would pack for an imaginary two-week trip and tuck away the rest out of sight (or to the back of your closet). Live off your "beach capsule" for the next while, and enjoy the liberating feeling of living with less. When you return from your pretend vacation, make note of how you felt with the selection you packed. Could you incorporate a more minimal mindset on permanent basis?

31

Go for a Windswept Look

Beauty routines are low maintenance and carefree on the beach. I didn't even pack a hair dryer for my visit to the cottage. Instead, I give my hair a break from the heat and let it dry "au naturel"! My laissez-faire approach creates a windswept, tousled style that people pay big money for at salons.

Embrace your natural beach waves by taking a break from the styling tools. When the weather permits, allow your hair to dry naturally. If your hair is prone to frizzies as mine is, there are lots of products on the market that can help. I use a drop of a product called *Olaplex No. 6 Bond Smoother* to tame things down. I sometimes put my hair up in a clip to dry. When I let it down, I'm left with beach wave perfection!

32

Exfoliate

A day at the beach is like visiting nature's spa. The salt water and sand work their magic on my skin. Walking barefoot on the sand for miles does wonders for the callouses on my feet. After just a few short days, they seem to melt away. No matter how hard I try, I can't keep the sheets from getting filled with sand, so I've decided to just embrace and accept it. Now each night feels like a full body exfoliation treatment!

Nothing feels more sensuous than smooth and silky skin. Most of us spend a lot of time, money and effort on our faces and forget the rest of our bodies. I once received a gift certificate for a sea salt and algae scrub at my favorite spa. It was divine, but also expensive. You can give yourself the royal beach spa treatment at home on a budget. Pick up a container of body scrub and allow yourself a few extra minutes in the shower to indulge. My favorite is *Rêve de Miel Deliciously Nourishing Body Scrub* by the French brand Nuxe. As the name implies (miel is honey in French), it smells decadent and delicious!

33

Take a Cinematic Adventure

In addition to being a beach lover, I am also a Francophile. I'm always seeking opportunities to bring a bit more French flair into my life. One of my favorite ways to do this is to watch movies set in France. (I force myself to shut off the subtitles to work on my language skills). If you haven't seen it, I highly recommend the movie *L'Odyssée*. It is a biographical adventure film that chronicles the life of the famous French ocean explorer, Jacques Cousteau. His life story is fascinating, and the underwater cinematography is spectacular and enchanting. (I award myself bonus points when I'm able to combine my love of the sea and the French culture.)

Just because you don't live by the sea doesn't mean you can't visit the beach often. The beach and the ocean are featured in countless films. No matter what genre you are into, I guarantee you'll be able to find one that gives you your beach fix. If you are into documentary films, I recommend *My Octopus Teacher*, an Academy Award winning film that chronicles the relationship that was forged between the filmmaker, Craig Foster, and a wild octopus. It's simply captivating!

34

Nap More

Naps are delicious. They are even more tasty when sprawled out on a lounge chair or beach blanket, the warm sun and wind caressing your skin. Beach naps come on so naturally. The soothing, tranquil and therapeutic atmosphere of the seaside lends itself to deep, guilt-free relaxation.

Such is not always the case at home. I think a lot of people associate naps with being lazy and unproductive. I disagree! I nap regularly and look for opportunities to sneak them in throughout my day. I find that they provide me an energizing and refreshing boost.

Nap more often and do so without guilt. If you find yourself drifting off on the couch on Sunday afternoon, don't fight it. Give your body the rest it craves. When you have a few moments of downtime in the car while waiting to pick up your kids, throw on your sunglasses and close your eyes. No one will even know what you're up to!

35

Seek Solitude

The beach can be a lonely place, which isn't necessarily a bad thing. The vast expanse of open space, the mournful sound of the foghorn and the cry of the gulls stir up sweet and sad emotions inside me. I welcome them all. As an introvert, I relish the sense of solitude the beach offers.

Whether you are an introvert, an extrovert or something in between, we all need alone time. Carve out time during your day where the only person you have to answer to is yourself. I rise as early as possible to make sure this need of mine is met. Getting an early start to the day allows me lots of alone time to think, journal and fit in my exercise. Having this time for myself helps me feel more grounded and present when the kids get up. I'm able to get them fed and out the door without feeling harried or rushed.

Could you set your alarm a half an hour earlier to give yourself a little extra time in the morning? I know this sounds crazy, but I get up at 5:00 AM. If that sounds painful to you, tack your alone time on at the end of the day. Retire to your bedroom early so you have the time and space to relax, read, take a bath and collect your thoughts.

36

Plant a Beach Inspired Garden

The beach is a harsh environment, but some plants seem to thrive there just the same. Coastal grasses are my favorite. I love the way their graceful, wispy leaves catch the wind and simulate the rippling of waves. The scent of wild beach roses is seductively heady and sweet. It is my definition of olfactory bliss. I'm also a fan of the delicate coastal shrub heather.

Add a beach vibe to your home garden by planting coastal inspired plants. Many of them are tough and will grow and thrive in a number of locations and hardiness zones. Sea thrift, sea holly, rugosa roses and blue fescue are some I've had the most luck with. Do your research and choose varieties that suit your climate.

If you don't have a garden, you can welcome that coastal feel indoors with house plants. Go tropical and pick yourself up a little palm tree!

37

Hydrate

Staying well-hydrated comes easily on the beach as quenching your thirst feels natural in this environment. It doesn't take long to feel parched when surrounded by sun, wind and salt, so I always keep a water bottle or tall glass of ice water close at hand. It helps, of course, that I'm free of distraction in this setting. Remembering to sip away on my refreshment is easy!

I can't say the same when I'm caught up in the hustle and bustle of daily life. It's a lot harder to remember to drink my recommended daily intake of water. Do you share in my struggle? There are lots of little tips and tricks you can try to help remember to stay hydrated. Keep a glass by the bathroom sink and start your day with a tall cold one (before you have a chance to get distracted). Invest in an attractive water bottle that is pleasant to sip from. Set a timer on your phone or watch as a reminder. Drink caffeine-free herbal tea. This counts towards your water intake and is a great alternative in the cold winter months.

38

Clear the Clutter

Our cottage is shared by four families on my mother's side, so it's really not possible for everyone to clutter up the space with their personal belongings. Each family has a designated spot in the attic to store their miscellaneous stuff. As a result, the cottage has a very clean, airy and spacious aesthetic, which is incredibly appealing and soothing. The clutter-free surroundings help maintain a clutter-free mindset!

Give your home a cottage-style makeover. Clear the clutter and free up both physical and mental space in the process. You don't have to get extreme and tackle the whole house at once à la Marie Kondo. Be patient with yourself and start with one room, or even one drawer or cupboard at a time.

When I'm in the mood to declutter I always begin with the coat closet off our mudroom. It's the first thing I see when I walk in the door, so it's a great feeling to have it sorted and organized. Because it holds our outerwear, it needs regular purging as the seasons change. It's also a space that all four members of our family share, so it can get untidy pretty quickly. What's your clutter hot spot? Make that the start line and then keep going.

39

Grab a Life Preserver

Although I've lived near the ocean all my life, you might be surprised to learn that I can barely swim. I definitely enjoy the water, but I'm more into wading and dipping than swimming laps. (Although I will say, if they ever decide to add the doggy paddle event to the Olympics, I will be a gold medalist.) The only time my lack of swimming skills becomes an issue is when I travel. Our family was in Guadeloupe a couple of years ago and my husband and kids were having so much fun snorkeling. I felt left out! The next day I went out and bought myself a snorkeling vest and finally ventured out to the reef with them. With my safety net in place, I was able to participate and enjoy the magic of the Caribbean Sea.

Face your fears, but don't be shy to set yourself up with a few safety nets to soften the blow if you fall. Certainly, when it comes to water, conquering your fears is not about being reckless. It would be foolish and dangerous to dive in over your head if you can't swim.

What are you scared to try? Have you always wanted to write a book? You might choose to release one under a pen name if you are feeling particularly timid. Do you want to visit an exotic location, but feel nervous because you aren't a seasoned traveler? Ask an experienced friend to tag along on the trip or book your vacation with a tour company. Don't let fear hold you back from accomplishing your goals.

40

Walk More

I participate in two main activities when I'm visiting my seaside retreat. When I'm not lounging, I'm walking. I alternate between the two depending on my mood and energy levels. I walk up and down the shoreline several times a day—sometimes solo, other times with company. Although I am an avid runner, I enjoy the slower pace of walks. They allow me to soak up the scenery in solitude or engage in a conversation with a companion.

Incorporate a walk into each day, even if you only have five or ten minutes to spare. It's a natural movement that feels good and gives you a chance to breathe in a healthy dose of fresh air. Morning is my favorite time of the day to walk, and I usually have a couple of companions tagging along (my little poodles Coco and Junior). When I worked as an accountant, I tried to make a point to get out and away from my desk during the lunch hour. I was lucky enough to work in a waterfront office building, so I had a taste of the ocean at my doorstep. Fit in a stroll wherever and whenever you can.

41

Sprinkle Your Home in Coastal Décor

The décor at the cottage exudes a minimal, airy and soothing vibe which mirrors the atmosphere of the beach just a few steps away. It provides the perfect balance between offering the comforts of home, while welcoming the outdoors in. The color scheme centers around the natural colors of the outdoor landscape. Seaside inspired scenes decorate the walls, while beach treasures of seashells and sea glass sit on display.

You don't have to live near the ocean to add elements of coastal décor to your home. There are many small and inexpensive touches that can provide your living space with that beachy vibe you are craving.

You can even select just one room that encompasses a seashore theme. The bathroom is an obvious choice!

When it comes to choosing a color palette, think soft and soothing—blue, gray, white, sand and sage green. As far as décor items, think natural materials: jute rugs, wicker baskets, cotton or linen throw cushions, weathered furniture, seashells, driftwood, rope, antique glass bottles (aqua shades are my favorite). If you are in the market for art, I have to mention that my cousin-in-law creates the most amazing works out of resin and acrylics. You can find her at www.kimberleyeddyfineart.com.

42

Dry Your Clothes on the Line

When I'm at the beach, I breathe more deeply. The fresh salty air provides me with a sense of calm, but also leaves me feeling invigorated. It has long been believed that seaside air boasts health benefits ranging from better sleep and digestion, to lower blood pressure. I'm not sure if there is science to support these claims, but I do know that a fresh sea breeze makes me happy!

If you want to welcome that clean air scent into your day-to-day life, dry your laundry outdoors whenever possible. I realize that clothes dryers aren't very popular in many parts of the world, but in North America they are ubiquitously overused. It only takes a few minutes longer to hang clothes on the line than to throw them in the dryer, and the benefits are worth the effort. Not only will you save energy and money, but your laundry will smell divine. You'll also get to spend some time outside, soaking up the sunshine. If nothing else, hang your sheets on the line. There's nothing like crawling in bed each night to the delicious and authentic scent of fresh air. They don't sell this stuff in a bottle!

43

Enjoy Lighter Meals

My appetite wanes on leisurely beach days. Perhaps it's the heat, or maybe it's just that I feel full to the brim with the beauty that surrounds me. My soul is satiated! Regardless of the reason, I naturally gravitate towards nibbly snacks and lighter meals during my stay at the cottage. No doubt some of this has to do with the fact that I'm mentally on vacation from the kitchen. I have no desire to devote much time to my culinary skills when the beach awaits me!

Listen to your body. It usually knows what is best for you. If you aren't particularly hungry, don't force feed yourself just because you've got a plate of food sitting in front of you. When your appetite is low, nourish yourself with fresh, light and wholesome meals that offer a healthy dose of vitamins without leaving you feeling overstuffed. Keep your fridge stocked with fresh produce and salad ingredients so you can whip up a light meal on a whim.

Since I eat a fairly hearty breakfast (it's my post-workout meal), I'm often not that hungry when lunch time rolls around. My go-to midday meal is a simple salad. The base is usually tender baby greens from the farmer's market, and then I toss in whatever I have on hand. I usually keep containers of cooked quinoa, lentils or beans in the fridge to add some substance to the meal. (I eat a plant-based diet, but diced chicken or tuna would be easy choices as well). I top the whole thing off with my favorite dressing and a small handful of nuts. (If you want to hear more about my salad bar approach, I elaborate further on it in my book, *Elevate Your Health*.)

44

Ebb and Flow with Grace

The tides are reliable and on time (right down to the minute). When I'm visiting the beach, I appreciate their punctuality as I can plan my activities accordingly. I always make sure I'm around for low tide, as I never miss a walk on the sandbars. The ebb and flow of life, on the other hand, doesn't operate on such a rigid schedule.

Embrace the ebbs and flows of life. When life flows, and it feels like everything is going your way, catch the wave! Capitalize on those times when you feel energized and bursting with enthusiasm. I'm in a state of flow right now writing this book. I just finished the final draft of a title about personal finance when I was ignited with the spark to dive into this manuscript. I actually set my money mindset book aside to follow the flow of my inspiration. I'll come back to it when the time feels right.

On the flip side, when life ebbs, and you feel yourself being pulled out to sea, give yourself grace. Release the urge to swim against the current. It only increases your sense of struggle. Last winter I was smack in the middle of writing a book when I injured my shoulder. I tried to soldier on typing at my computer, but in the end, I had to recognize that I was in a lot of pain. Denying and fighting it was making things worse. What my body needed was rest, ice and time to heal. I put the book aside, and revisited when my flow and health returned.

45

Travel by Book

While I do love to travel occasionally, I'm a homebody by nature. Visiting the beachside family cottage each year provides the best of both worlds. It serves as a getaway, but also feels like a second home. I've travelled to this place every summer for the past forty-seven years! When I can't visit in person, I reach for the next best thing—a beach inspired read.

Books provide my favorite form of travel when the real thing is out of reach. They allow you to transport yourself to a far-off land, anytime, anywhere and for just a few dollars (or free if you make use of your local library). Beach themed reading is really a genre on its own, and there are endless titles to choose from.

Whether you are into romance, mystery or non-fiction, you will be able to get your beach fix on the bookshelf.

A recent favorite of mine is *Where the Crawdads Sing* by Delia Owens. It combines romance, crime and mystery, but also serves as an informal nature reference. The author holds a BSc in zoology and a PhD in animal behavior, so her descriptions of the natural world and coastal life are meticulous and enthralling. I lost myself in this story, and never wanted it to end.

46

Create Mystery

The beach has long been cloaked in a sense of mystery. Tales of pirates, hidden treasure and souls lost at sea intrigue us and draw us in. Every few years I stumble across a message in a bottle, and I squeal with excitement when I do. I have to admit, I've yet to find one that contained anything extraordinary. I've always imagined it would be fun to be the one to discover the missing piece to a puzzle, and perhaps play a hand in the reuniting of two long lost lovers. Maybe someday!

Embrace a sense of mystery in your own day-to-day. Find ways to add a touch of intrigue, romance and deliciousness to your life. Wear exquisite lingerie underneath your blue jeans, read romance novels, watch old mystery movies, spritz yourself in an enchanting perfume, kiss your partner passionately at an unexpected moment, exercise restraint in conversations (note to self: stop blabbering), wear oversized sunglasses, decorate your home with fresh flowers, light candles. Lastly, next time you do visit the oceanside, why not toss your own message in a bottle out to sea? Give the gift of mystery back to the universe.

47

Sleep Deeply

I sleep like a log at the beach. I'm guessing it is a combination of factors that contribute to my nights of high-quality rest. Obviously, I'm on vacation when I visit the cottage, so I'm usually in a pretty relaxed state of mind. I try not to pack my worries in my suitcase! Being outdoors, active and immersed in fresh air all day probably helps tire me out as well (in a good way). Lastly, as I mentioned in chapter 12, I'm lucky enough to be lulled to sleep by the sound of ocean waves. Bedtime doesn't get much dreamier than that!

Proper and sufficient rest is important to your health, so it's a no brainer to try to improve the quality of your sleep. I'm always tweaking my bedtime routine to create a more blissful, restful atmosphere. First off, get comfortable. Treat yourself to the most decadent sheets you can afford. You only really need one high quality set as you can leave the bed stripped while you wash them. I keep a second emergency set on hand in the linen closet, but barely use it.

Sleep meditations are a great way to clear and soothe your mind before you drift off. (My husband and I call them "beditations".) Choose one that features the sounds of the ocean and pretend you have escaped to your very own seaside retreat.

Lastly, make sure you get enough exercise during the day. Move your body so it naturally wants to slip into a blissful state of rest when bedtime rolls around.

48

Eat High Quality Ice Cream

Beach treats are fun and refreshing, especially those of the frosty and frozen variety. My mother plays fairy grandmother to my children, and keeps the cottage freezer stocked with popsicles and ice cream sandwiches. (My dad is sure to help himself to his fair share of the stash.) I don't indulge in treats often, but of course I make an exception on vacation. When I do choose to spoil myself, I'm discerning with my selection. I like my ice cream to be of high quality. (Yes, I consider myself mostly vegan, but I do make exceptions when it comes to dessert!) I'm actually more of a *gelato* kind of girl. I'd rather have one small scoop of something exquisite, than scarf down the entire tub of a substandard variety.

Indulge in a beach inspired treat now and then and savor every bite (or lick). Choose quality over quantity. Your taste buds and your waistline will thank you. Instead of grabbing a bowl and spoon, opt for cone instead, even if you are just at home. Admit it, cones are just more fun, playful and reminiscent of childhood. They also encourage smaller servings. One single decadent scoop is the perfect topping for a cone.

49

Get Outside

Beach days run from dawn until dusk, and often beyond if it's a good night for a bonfire and marshmallows. I slip into the cottage for bathroom breaks and to grab a snack, but other than that, you'll find me on the beach. I want to maximize my time in this special place. No matter what's on the agenda, my motto is, "Take it outside." My daily activities include reading, walking, journaling, beachcombing, snoozing, chatting, running, kayaking and doggy paddling. Life is just better on the beach!

Spend more time in nature. It doesn't matter if it's the beach, the forest, the countryside, a marshland or the desert. So many of us live lives that are removed from the natural world. As we go about our busy days, it's easy to forget about the beauty that is available to us just outside the boxes of our homes and office buildings. I'm lucky enough to live in a rural area, and most of my days include at least one short walk through the forested trails around our property. Even if you live in a large urban center, you can take advantage of the nature opportunities in your community by visiting local parks and greenspaces. At a minimum, find a quiet bench to sit on while you admire the birds and listen to the leaves rustling in the wind. I think we often forget that as humans, we are in fact animals. We too are part of the natural world, so tap into those animal instincts and get outside!

50

Immerse Yourself

Although I'm not much of a swimmer, I never miss my daily dip when I'm visiting the cottage. Rain, or shine, I don my bathing suit and wade out into nature's bathtub. Immersing myself in the cool water feels refreshing, therapeutic and invigorating. It makes me feel alive!

What makes *you* feel alive? What captivates your curiosity? What ignites you with energy and enthusiasm? Immerse yourself in your passions. Allow yourself to become completely absorbed in something that fills you up and feeds your soul. In my book, *Elevate the Everyday*, I discuss the concept of the dreamy/practical list. I suggest you create to-do lists that incorporate both practical tasks, as well as dreamy activities. By scheduling time for your dreams, you are making a commitment to yourself to pursue what you are most passionate about. Are you fascinated with Italian culture? Sign up for weekly Italian lessons, and surround yourself in Italian cuisine, literature, music and art. Do you love classic literature? Set yourself up for an ambitious reading challenge and schedule an hour a day to get through your reading list.

For the past two years, writing has become my passion. When I come up with a new book idea, I completely immerse myself in the writing process. I slip into an inspired state where the words just seem to flow from my fingertips. The more time I spend absorbed in my writing, the more energized and alive I feel.

Bonus:
Find Joy in Simplicity

As my time on the beach draws to a close, I take one last stroll down to the water's edge and fill my lungs with a deep breath of salt-tinged air. I want to savor everything about this moment, allowing the sights, sounds and sensations to soak into my pores and permeate my being. I feel full to the brim with gratitude. This week has replenished my soul and left me with a great sense of abundance and satisfaction. The stark simplicity of the beach reminds me that I need very little in life to feel fulfilled and happy.

Take stock of your life and *identify what is most important to you*. What brings you the greatest joy? What fills you up inside? What do you value most above all else? When I walked through this exercise, I realized that the value of the intangible goods in my life far outweighs the tangible. Family, friends, love, community, good health, warmth, good food, great sleep, a sense of purpose, time to explore my passions… when these needs and wants are met, I crave less of all the other stuff (a new car, designer clothes, a new kitchen countertop, exotic vacations).

I suggest you take the time to put pen to paper and collect your thoughts in a journal. (There is great value in actually writing things down instead of just making a mental list.) When you are done, sit back and really absorb the words you came up with. Breathe them in. Let them soak in and settle in your chest. Notice how you feel when you realize that you *already have* so much of what truly makes you happy in life. Embrace this sense of appreciation, and just as you would with that glistening seashell you discover on the shoreline, slip it into your back pocket. Pull it out any time you need a little reminder of the beauty and abundance in your life.

A Note from The Author

Thank you so much for joining me on this little excursion to the beach. I hope that you were able to collect a few seashells of inspiration to slip into your own pockets. The beach has many wise lessons to teach us, and I trust I've convinced you that you don't have to live on or near the seaside to embrace them into your everyday life. Living a beach inspired life is available to each and every one of us.

Capturing the essence of the beach is really about seeking more of what we instinctively crave and thrive on in life—simplicity, peace, tranquility, freedom, connection, self-care, adventure, nature and fresh air. What's so amazing and exciting, is that each and every one of these things is free, and yours for the taking. It's really about shifting your mindset and tracking down the hidden seashells life has to offer.

If you enjoyed my writing, please check out some of my other books, which are all available on Amazon.

They cover a wide range of lifestyle topics including personal style, beauty routines, household management, home décor, travel, fitness, personal finances, health, food, attitude…and so much more!

I also have a tiny favor to ask. If you enjoyed this book, I would greatly appreciate it if you would take a moment and leave a review on Amazon. As a self-published author, reviews are incredibly valuable and helpful. They allow me to gain feedback on my writing, spread the word about my books, and connect with my wonderful readers!

I wish you lots of luck and success in living a peaceful, connected, fulfilling and magical beach inspired life. It's time for us to say goodbye, but maybe I'll see you on the beach!

Much love,

Jennifer

Other Books by Jennifer Melville

Elevate the Everyday:
Actions and Ideas to Enhance the Experience of Daily Life

Elevate Your Personal Style:
Inspiration for the Everyday Woman

Elevate Your Health:
Inspiration and Motivation to Embrace and Maintain a
Healthy Lifestyle

Elevate Your Life at Home:
Inspiring Ideas to Add Joy, Peace and Magic to Your Homelife

Preloved Chic:
Stylish Secrets to Elevate Your Wardrobe
With Second-Hand Fashion

Paris in my Panties:
Live Your Best (French Inspired) Life

About the Author

Jennifer Melville is a self-published author. She decided to embark on a writing career because she wanted to tap into a community of like-minded individuals who share in her enthusiasm for living well and seeking ways to elevate daily life. She is a professional accountant by trade, who approaches life with an analytical and observant mind. Jennifer has been exploring the concept of elevating the everyday for over twenty years. She is passionate about family, health, fitness, fashion, nutrition, nature and all the beauty life has to offer.

Jennifer lives by the sea in beautiful Nova Scotia, Canada with her husband, two sons and little poodles Coco and Junior.

You can connect with her by email, on her blog, or on her Instagram page.

jenniferlynnmelville@gmail.com
www.theelevatedeveryday.com
www.instagram.com/the.elevated.everyday

Printed in Great Britain
by Amazon